SWU-700-007

UNIFORMS OF RUSSIAN ARMY OF ELIZABETH OF RUSSIA VOL.1

UNDER THE REIGN OF ELIZABETH PETROVNA FROM 1741 TO 1761, AND PETER III FROM 1762

From the Viskovatov's greatest work:
"Historical description of the clothing and
arms of the Russian Army"

SOLDIERSHOP PUBLISHING

AUTHOR

Aleksandr Vasilevich Viskovatov born 22 April (4 May New Style) 1804, died 27 February (11 March) 1858 in St. Petersburg, Russian military historian. He graduated from the 1st Cadet Corps and served in the artillery, the hydrographic depot of the Naval Ministry, and then in the Department of Military Educational Institutions. He mainly studied historical artifacts and the histories of military units. Viskovatov's greatest work was the Historical Description of the Clothing and Arms of the Russian Army.

Title: **UNIFORMS OF RUSSIAN ARMY OF ELIZABETH OF RUSSIA VOL. 1 -**
Under the reign of Elizabeth Petrovna from 1741 to 1761 and Peter III from 1762
By A.V.Viskovatov. Serie edit by Luca S. Cristini. First edition by Soldiershop. February 2018
Cover & Art Design: Luca S. Cristini. Plates re-colorations by Anna Cristini.
ISBN code: 978-88-93273183

Published by Soldiershop publishing, via Padre Davide, 7 - 24050 Zanica (BG) ITALY. www.soldiershop.com

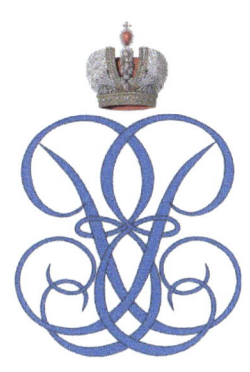

UNIFORMS
OF THE RUSSIAN ARMY OF
ELIZABETH OF RUSSIA
1741-1762
VOL. 1

UNDER THE REIGN OF ELIZABETH PETROVNA
FROM 1741 TO 1761 AND PETER III FROM 1762

HISTORICAL DESCRIPTION OF THE CLOTHING AND ARMS OF THE RUSSIAN ARMY - A.V. VISKOVATOV

Soldiershop is glad to presents the complete collection of the great job made by A.V. Viskovatov dedicated to the uniforms and weapons belonging from the first Zar and Russian emperors to the Russian army during the Napoleonic period, until 1860 about. The time we considered in this volume corresponds to the reigns of of the Duke of Courland and Princess Anna of Braunschweig-Luneburg from 1740 to 1741, Empress Elizabeth Petrovna from 1741 to 1761, and Emperor Peter III from 1762.

Our new edition, the first ever published in English, both on paper and digital format, boasts a large number of color plates, many of them unpublished and re-coloured by our team of expert artists and scholars of uniformology. Each volume is based on 100 color plates or more, always accompanied by the original translated text which describes the subjects of the plates.

A unique work in its genre, a must have in any respecting collection!

Aleksandr Vasilevich Viskovatov born 22 April (4 May New Style) 1804, died 27 February (11 March) 1858 in St. Petersburg, Russian military historian. He graduated from the 1st Cadet Corps and served in the artillery, the hydrographic depot of the Naval Ministry, and then in the Department of Military Educational Institutions.

He mainly studied historical artifacts and the histories of military units. Viskovatov's greatest work was the Historical Description of the Clothing and Arms of the Russian Army (Vols. 1-30, St. Petersburg, 1841-62; 2nd ed. Vols. 1-34, St. Petersburg - Novosibirsk - Leningrad, 1899-1948). This work is based on a great quantity of archival documents and contains four thousand colored illustrations.

Viskovatov was the author of Chronicles of the Russian Army (Books 1-20, St. Petersburg, 1834-42) and Chronicles of the Russian Imperial Army (Parts 1-7, St. Petersburg, 1852). He collected valuable material on the history of the Russian navy which went into A Short Overview of Russian Naval Campaigns and General Voyages to the End of the XVII Century (St. Petersburg, 1864; 2nd edition Moscow, 1946). Together with A.I. Mikhailovskii-Danilevskii he helped prepare and create the Military Gallery in the Winter Palace.

He wrote the historical military inscriptions for the walls of the Hall of St. George in the Great Palace of the Kremlin. (From the article in the Soviet Military Encyclopedia.)

◄ *Elizabeth of Russia by Georg Christoph Grooth*

CONTENTS

*

HISTORICAL DESCRIPTION OF THE RUSSIAN ARMY AND HIS BATTLES IN THE SEVEN YEARS' WAR

THE RUSSIAN ARMY IN THE XVIII CENTURY

During the Petr the Great era the amount of Russian army was of 200.000 men, by 1756 the army had increased to 331.000. Of this about 175.000 men belonged in to regular army, 75.000 were the troops of garrison, 28.000 in the militia, 13.000 in artillery and engineers corps. Finally, about 45.000 men are tin the irregular troops. From this sum we deduct the Imperial Guards, which remained in St. Petersburg during any war, the really amount of available army had only some 130.000 men, to cover the immense Russian empire...

After Peter the Great, the founder of Russian army the life of a noble officer was strictly prescribed: From 7 to 20 years old to be spent in study, and those from 20 to 45 in military time! The army recruiting was confined to the ten provinces of Russian empire. Every man was called to reinforced the army, but some "people" may spent his money to provide a substitute.

Once in military uniform the recruit had small possibility of ever seeing his home and family again. Only when he was too old, also for garrison service, he was given a small pension for the last years. The discipline of the Russian army was always very severe, but at least, under the Empress Elizabeth the death penalty had been abolished. The result of this state was that in 1756 with about 130.000 men serving in the army, only 190 are recorded as having deserted.

The Russian cavalry consisted of the Horse Guards and Garde du corps for the elite units. 3 cuirassier regiments and 29 dragoons regiments.

From 1756 the number of cuirassier regiment was increased to five. But during the campaign operation only 14 cavalry regiment were employed, with the remainder in Russia to control barracks and towns. The irregular cavalry consisted of several Hussar regiments, all based on foreign recruits. Also, are in service several corps of Russian Cossacks (about 20.000 men enlisted).

The infantry of the Guard consisted in 3 regiments. The line was based on 41 regiments.

As the cavalry, only 32 of this regiment was employed in the war in 1756. During the time of seven years' war, the Russian infantry was recorded for a great tenacity, equal and sometimes superior to that of Prussian army!

The artillery of Russia in 1756was the subject of very important reforms, and from the 1757 it receives various new modern weapon (guns and howitzer). This fact gave to the Russian artillery a predominant and great role in all the battles of the seven years war.

From 1756 in the Russian army every infantry regiment had his artillery attached units, consisting in two small guns and four mortars. The field artillery instead is based on about 250 weapons in five different calibres, was formed various brigades of 20 guns each. Usually as several other nations of XVIII century, Russian army was plagued with a big and heavy military train. In 1757 it has about 6.000 different vehicles, which required about a third of the men of the army to handl

.The Russian uniform, with the exclusion of the hussars and Cossack are simply dressed (for the time) in French style.

Elizabeth at horse in military uniform with black Servant by Grooth (1743, Hermitage)

THE BATTLE OF RUSSIAN ARMY IN THE SEVEN YEARS' WAR

During the Seven Years' War, the **Battle of Gross-Jägersdorf** of 30 August 1757 was one of the first victory for the Russian force under Field Marshal Stepan Fedorovich Apraksin over a smaller Prussian force commanded by Field Marshal Hans von Lehwaldt. This was the first battle in which Russia engaged during the Seven Years' War. Despite the tactical success, supply problems made a successful advance further into East Prussia impractical.

Apraksin decided not to take Königsberg and ordered a withdrawal soon after the battle. Suspecting collusion between Apraksin and Chancellor Alexey Bestuzhev-Ryumin, who had opposed the invasion, Elizabeth of Russia removed Apraksin from command, ordered Bestuzhev-Ryumin to face trial for treason, and appointed William Fermor as the head of the army.

Femor led the army back into East Prussia in the following year. Although the Seven Years' War was a global conflict, it took a specific intensity in the European theater based on the recently concluded War of the Austrian Succession (1740–1748). The 1748 Treaty of Aix-la-Chapelle gave Frederick II of Prussia, known as Frederick the Great, the prosperous province of Silesia. Empress Maria Theresa of Austria had signed the treaty to gain time to rebuild her military forces and forge new alliances; she was intent upon regaining ascendancy in the Holy Roman Empire as well as the Silesian province. In 1754, escalating tensions between Britain and France in North America offered France an opportunity to break the British dominance of Atlantic trade.

Seeing the opportunity to regain her lost territories and to limit Prussia's growing power, Austria put aside the old rivalry with France to form a new coalition.

Faced with this turn of events, Britain aligned herself with the Kingdom of Prussia; this alliance drew in not only the British king's territories held in personal union, including Hanover, but also those of his relatives in the Electorate of Brunswick-Lüneburg and the Landgraviate of Hesse-Kassel. This series of political maneuvers became known as the Diplomatic Revolution. At the outset of the war, Frederick had one of the finest armies in Europe: his troops—any company—could fire at least four volleys a minute, and some of them could fire five. By the end of 1757, the course of the war had gone well for Prussia, and poorly for Austria.

Prussia had achieve spectacular victories at Rossbach and Leuthen and reconquered parts of Silesia that had fallen back to Austria. The Prussians then pressed south into Austrian Moravia.

In April 1758, Prussia and Britain concluded the Anglo-Prussian Convention in which the British committed to pay Frederick an annual subsidy of £670,000. Britain also dispatched 7,000–9,000 troops to reinforce Frederick's brother-in-law, the Duke Ferdinand of Brunswick-Wolfenbüttel's army. Ferdinand evicted the French from Hanover and Westphalia and re-captured the port of Emden in March 1758; he crossed the Rhine, causing general alarm in France.

Despite Ferdinand's victory over the French at the Battle of Krefeld and the brief occupation of Düsseldorf, successful maneuvering of larger French forces required him to withdraw across the Rhine.

While Ferdinand and the English allies kept the French busy in the Rhineland, Prussia had to contend with Sweden, Russia, and Austria. There remained a possibility that Prussia could lose Silesia to Austria, Pomerania to Sweden, Magdeburg to Saxony, and East Prussia to Poland or Russia: an entirely nightmarish scenario.- In particular, East Prussia was cut off from the rest of Prussia by 500 kilometers (311 mi) of Polish territory, and seemed an easy target, but some Russian court of-

▲▶ The battle of Gross-Jägersdorf of 30 August 1757

ficials—notably Chancellor Alexey Bestuzhev-Ryumin—opposed Russia's entry into what seemed like a largely western European dispute. Bestuzhev-Ryumin did not trust the Prussians, but also had little liking for the French or the British. In this conflict, which grew out of the major realignment of European power diplomacy, it was difficult to determine if the enemy of an enemy was a friend.

DISPOSITIONS

The Russian field marshal Stepan Fyodorovich Apraksin commanded an army of approximately 55,000 men and crossed the Niemen. They captured Memel, which became the army's base for an invasion of the rest of Prussia. Apraxin was cautious, however, and inexperienced in wartime measures. Instead of marching on Wehlau, as was expected, he ordered his forces to cross the Pregel River in safety, near the village of Gross-Jägersdorf.

The position in East Prussia had stretched the Russian supply lines, and the troops were forced to forage. Foraging quickly degenerated into unruliness and turned into a scorched earth policy, a process that Frederick derided, thinking the Russians undisciplined troops; a disciplined army, the King reasoned, would make quick work of them.

They moved on Königsberg, to try to take or at least invest the city. Frederick sent his 70-year-old Field Marshal Hans von Lehwaldt, who commanded of forces in East Prussia, with 28,000 men; he supplied Lehwaldt with one hundred officers' patents to fill as he saw fit, expecting him to strengthen the army there. He also sent ambiguous orders to take on the Russians whenever his field marshal saw fit. Frederick had not given him specific instructions, just general ones to act when the moment seemed propitious.

BATTLE

The Russians started the day with a leisurely march, but the army was undisciplined and difficult to move in any concentrated, organized way. Seeing the opportunity, the Prussians attacked the milling and "unprepared mob" of Russian soldiers. Lehwaldt's cavalry attacked the northern and southern flanks of the Russian army, inflicting initial heavy losses. The Russians, entirely unprepared for an assault by an army half its size, degenerated into further confusion. Apraxin's inexperienced commanders tried to organize the infantry; General Pyotr Rumyantsev, who later became one of Russia's best generals, managed to rally the Russians in the center, as it recovered from the shock of the initial attack. General Vasily Lopukhin

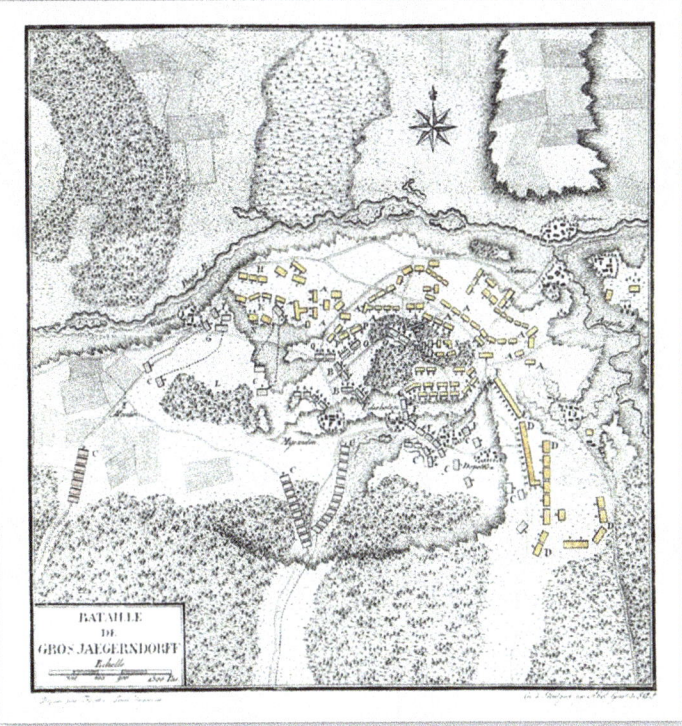

was bayoneted by the Prussians: some reports say he died in the arms of his comrades, others, that he died a few days later. Initially, Lehwaldt's force retained some advantage in the battle. The fierce Prussian assault prevented the Russians from forming the traditional squares with which to repel cavalry, but they did not break and run. Furthermore, observers reported that the main force of Prussians advancing on the center fired volley upon volley with their usual ruthless efficiency. Russian army recovered from the shock of the initial assault and counter-attacked. Initially mesmerized by the Prussian onslaught, the Russians recovered to shoot back; their return fire was not of the same efficiency, but it was nevertheless effective and the Prussian line eventually collapsed under it. Furthermore, the Kalmyk cavalry and the Don Cossacks, on the Prussian left, pretended to retreat so as to trap the attacking Prussians under heavy artillery fire.

This was an effort by Apraksin to encircle the Prussians with his larger army, which Lehwaldt was able to avoid. Lehwaldt's force retired to its former camp and held its ground there.

AFTERMATH

The Prussians achieved a surprise attack, seized a number of positions from numerically superior forces and inflicted equivalent losses. As at Zorndorf, they proved to be effective against stronger forces in close-quarter fighting. On the other hand, the Russians, as a Saxon officer remarked, "had neither time nor opportunity to form a square, and yet they did extremely well", despite being taken completely by surprise. Lehwaldt lost between 4,600 and 5,000 casualties and Apraxin, approximately 5,400. Some sources estimate Russian losses as higher: perhaps half again as many casualties, so in the 7,000 range. Although Lehwaldt withdrew his corps from the battle, and subsequently oversaw the Blockade of Stralsund. The Russian success at Gross-Jägersdorf also encouraged Sweden to join the fight against Prussia.

KUNERSDORF

The decisive **Battle of Kunersdorf** occurred on 12 August 1759 near Kunersdorf (Kunowice), immediately east of Frankfurt an der Oder (the second largest city in Prussia). Part of the Third Silesian War and the wider Seven Years' War, the battle involved over 100,000 men. An Allied army commanded by Pyotr Saltykov and Ernst Gideon von Laudon that included 41,000 Russians and 18,500 Austrians defeated Frederick the Great's army of 50,900 Prussians.

The terrain complicated battle tactics for both sides, but the Russians and the Austrians, having arrived in the area first, were able to overcome many of its difficulties by strengthening a causeway between two small ponds. They had also devised a solution to Frederick's deadly *modus operandi*, the oblique order. Although Frederick's troops initially gained the upper hand in the battle, the sheer number of Allied troops gave the Russians and Austrians an advantage.

By afternoon, when the combatants were exhausted, fresh Austrian troops thrown into the fray secured the Allied victory. This was the only time in the Seven Years' War that the Prussian Army, under Frederick's direct command, disintegrated into an undisciplined mass.

With this loss, Berlin, only 80 kilometers (50 mi) away, lay open to assault by the Russians and Austrians. Saltykov and Laudon did not follow up on the victory. Only 3,000 soldiers from Frederick's original 50,000 remained with him after the battle, although many more had simply scattered and rejoined the army within a few days.

This represented the penultimate success of the Russian Empire under Elizabeth of Russia and was arguably Frederick's worst defeat.

TERRAIN

The terrain surrounding Kunersdorf suited itself better to defense than offense. Between the Frankfurt dam, a long earthen bulwark that helped to contain the Oder river, and to the north of Kunersdorf itself stretched a 3 km (2 mi) line of knolls; Judenberge (Jews Hill), Mühlberge (Mill Hill) and Walkberge (also spelled Walckberge).

None was more than 30 m (98 ft) high. The hillocks were steeper on the north side than the south, but bounded by a marshy, boggy meadow called the Elsbusch, or the Alder wasteland.

East of Kunersdorf and the Walkberge, the Hühner Fleiss (*Fleiss* means running water) was joined by another stream that tumbled between two more hillocks.

Past the Walkberge and beyond the Hühner stood two more promontories at Trettin.

Several ravines intersected the ridge of hillocks: starting at the northeastern end, the Bäckergrund joined the Hühner Fleiss. Just east of the Walkberge a small ravine separated the Walkberge from the Mühlberge. Another narrow roadway cut through the Mühlberge ridge, then a second narrow depression, known as the Kuhgrund (cow hollow), lay west of that.

Beyond the Kuhgrund, the ground rose again, then dipped into a fourth hollow in which lay a Jewish settlement known as a shtetl, and the ground rose into the Judenberge; from this point, one could overlook most of Frankfurt and its suburbs.

To the southeast lay a variety of small promontories, called the Grosser- and Kleiner- Spitzberge. Like the northwest side of the ridge, this ground was covered with small ponds, streams, marshy fields, and broad meadows. Natural features—ponds, causeways, swamps—would restrict wide movements

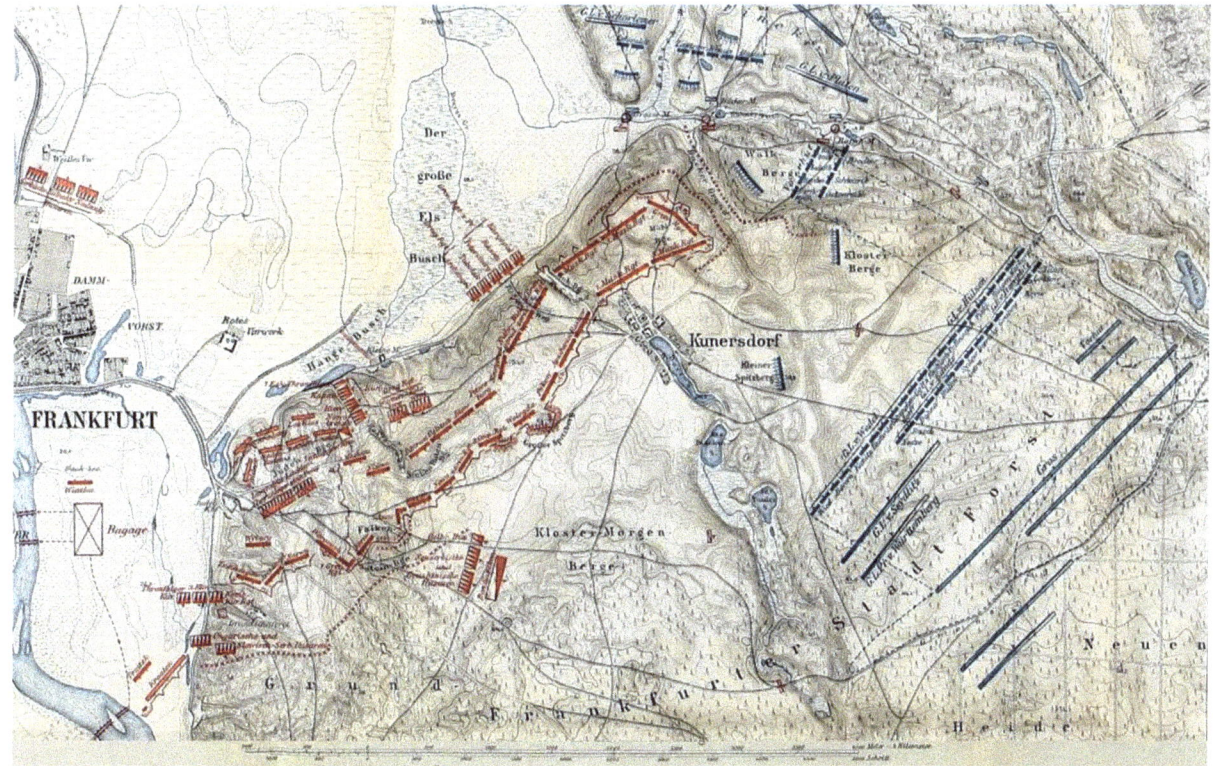

Battle of Kunersdorf: Russian troops are shown in dark red; Prussian troops are in blue. Map by German Grosser Generalstab (General Staff), Wars of Frederick the Great. 1880.

on some of the terrain. To the east and north of the entire landscape lay the Forest of Reppen. Here the ground itself was sandy and unstable. The scrub forests were threaded with streams, springs, and bogs of all kinds.

ALLIED DISPOSITIONS

Sources vary greatly on the relative strength of the Russian and Austrian armies. Saltykov had started the summer with a force of about 60,000 men; he had lost close to 4,000 at the Battle of Kay. Laudon had been detached from the main Austrian army with 22–24,000 men, and sent north to support the Russian cause.

A portion of the Russian force remained in Frankfurt as the Allied advanced guard. Saltykov had expected the Austrian commander-in-chief's entire army to arrive; instead a mere wing under Laudon's command came to his aid. Their collaboration was complicated by their personalities.

Neither Laudon nor Saltykov had great command of operational arts. Saltykov did not like foreigners; Laudon thought Saltykov was inscrutable. Neither liked conversing through translators, and both mistrusted each other's intentions.

Laudon wanted a fight, so he swallowed his differences and joined the Russians in building fortifications. Saltykov established his troops on a strong position from which to receive the Prussian attack, concentrating his force in the center, which he calculated was the best way to counter-act any attempt by Frederick to deploy his deadly oblique order. Saltykov entrenched himself in a position running from the Judenberge through the Grosser Spitzberge to the Mühlberge, creating a bristling line of fortifications, and faced his troops to the northwest; the Judenberge, most heavily fortified, fronted what he believed would be Frederick's approach.

He and the Austrian troops were stretched along the ridge that ran from the outskirts of Frankfurt to just north of the village of Kunersdorf. Anticipating that Frederick would rely on his cavalry, the Russians effectively negated any successful cavalry charge by using fallen trees to break up the ground on the approaches.

Saltykov had little concern about the extreme northwestern face of the ridge, which was steep and fronted by the marshy Elsbruch, but a few of the Austrian contingents faced northwest as a precaution. He expected Frederick to attack him from the west, from Frankfurt, and from the Frankfurt outer city. The Russians constructed redans and flèche to protect all the potentially weak points of their fortifications; they built glacis to cover the most shallow of the hills, and scarps and counterscarps to protect seemingly weak points. Abatis not only littered the hillsides, but dotted flat ground. By 10 August, his scouts had told him that Frederick was at the far western edge of Frankfurt. Accordingly, Saltykov took everything he could from the city by way of sustenance, all oxen, sheep, chickens, produce, wine, beer, in a flurry of ransacking.

PRUSSIAN PLANS

While Saltykov plundered the city and prepared for Frederick's assault from the west, the Prussians reached Reitwein, some 28 km (17 mi) north of Frankfurt on 10 August, and built pontoon bridges during the night. Frederick crossed the Oder in the night and the next morning, and moved southward toward Kunersdorf; the Prussians established a staging area near Göritz (also spelled Gohritz on the old maps), about 9.5 km (6 mi) north-northeast of Kunersdorf late on 11 August with about 50,000 men; of these, 2,000 were deemed unfit for service and stayed behind to guard the baggage.

Frederick conducted a perfunctory reconnaissance of his enemy's position, accompanied by a forest ranger and an officer who had previously been stationed in Frankfurt. He also consulted a peasant who, though garrulous, was uninformed about military needs: the peasant told the King that a natural obstacle between the Red Grange (a large farmstead between Kunersdorf and Frankfurt's outer city) and Kunersdorf was unpassable; what the peasant did not know was that the Russians had been there long enough to construct a causeway linking these two sections.

Looking to the east through his telescope, Frederick saw some wooded hills, called the Reppen Forest, and he believed he could use them to screen an advance, much like he had done at Leuthen. He did not send scouts to reconnoiter the land or question locals about the ground in the forest.

Furthermore, through his glass he could see that the Russians were facing west and north, and their fortifications were stronger on the west.

He decided that *all* the Allies were facing northwest and that the forest was readily passable. After his perfunctory reconnaissance, Frederick returned to his camp to develop his battle plan. He planned to direct a diversionary force, commanded by Finck, to the Hühner Fliess, to demonstrate in front of what he believed to be the main Russian line. He would march with his main army to the southeast of the Allied position, circling around Kunersdorf, screened by the Reppen Forest.

This way, he thought, he would surprise his enemy, forcing the Allied army to reverse fronts, which is a complicated maneuver for even the best trained troops. Frederick could then employ his much feared oblique battle order, feinting with his left flank as he did so. Ideally, this would allow him to roll up the Allied line from the Mühlberge.

FINAL DISPOSITIONS

Late in the afternoon on the 11th, wily Saltykov realized that Frederick was not advancing on him from Frankfurt, and changed his plans. He inverted his flanks: instead of having the left wing at the shtetl and the right at Mühlberge, he reversed his flank with the right at the shtetl.

Then the Russians set fire to Kunersdorf. Within hours, the only thing left was the stone church and some walls. While Frederick developed his plan to outflank Saltykov by maneuvering behind him, Saltykov outfoxed him.

BATTLE

Prussian activities began at 2:00 am on 12 August. Troops were roused and, within the hour, they set off. Finck's corps had the shortest distance to travel, and the five brigades arrived at the assigned post, the high ground northeast of the Walkeberge, by dawn; Karl Friedrich von Moller established the artillery park on the highest ground at Trettin, and pointed it at the Walkberge, on the hills north of the Hühner Fleiss.

Finck's infantry and cavalry demonstrated in front of the five Russian regiments as a diversion, while the remainder of Frederick's army continued in a 37 km (23 mi) semi-circle around the eastern flank of the Russian line, to approach from the village from the southeast.

The grueling march took up to eight hours. Frederick intended to flank his opposition, and attack what he assumed would be its weakest side, but again, he sent no reconnaissance, not a single hussar or dragoon, to confirm his assumptions.

Mid-way in the march, Frederick finally realized that he would end up facing his enemy, instead of approaching from behind. Furthermore, a row of ponds forced him to break his line into three narrow columns, exposing it to full Russian fire power. Frederick changed his dispositions; the Prussian right vanguard would concentrate east of the ponds of Kunersdorf and make an assault on the Mühlberge.

Frederick calculated that he could turn the Austrian-Russian flank, and push the Russians off the Mühlberge heights. His redeployment took time, and the apparent hesitation in the assault confirmed to Saltykov what Frederick planned; he moved more troops around so that the strongest line would face the Prussian onslaught.

Frederick's army became bogged down in the Reppen Forest. The day was already hot and sultry, and the men were already tired. The trees were thick and the ground was unstable and oozy in some parts, which made the movement of the heavy guns difficult. Delay after delay slowed them down.

The carriages pulling the biggest guns, traveling with the bulk of the army, were too wide to cross the narrow forest bridges and the columns had to be reshuffled in the woods.

The Russians could hear them, but thought they were scouting parties, albeit noisy ones; they calculated Finck's column was the primary force. Between 5:00 am. and 6:00 am., only Finck's demonstrating corps, to the north by Trettin, were visible to the Russians. Finck's right wing moved out of the hills toward the mill on Hühner Fleiss; more Prussians from Finck's left and center prepared to attack the Walkberge.

Finck's artillery awaited Frederick's signal, but the bulk of Frederick's army still crashed about in the woods. Finally, at 8:00 am., some of Frederick's army emerged from the woods, with most of Generalleutnant Friedrich Wilhelm von Seydlitz's cavalry and the rest of his artillery; a short time later, the rest of the Prussians emerged from the woods, and the Russians realized it was not a scouting party, but the main army. The Prussians stood ranked for battle, which now began in earnest.

Finck's artillery park had been in place since dawn and, at 11:30 am, Moller initiated bombardment of the Russian position from the northern and northeastern ends of the Russian line (now the Russian left). In error, the Russian artillery had faced their batteries to the meadows beyond the Mühlberge, not the ravine, and had to be reset. For 30 minutes, the two sides bombarded each other.

At about noon, Frederick sent his first wave of soldiers toward the Russian position on the Mühlberge. Frederick favored mixed troops in such conditions, and his forward troops included grenadiers and musketeers, and some cuirassiers. The Prussian artillery batteries created an arc of fire on the Russian sector by the Walkberge and the Kleiner Spitzberge; the infantry could safely move under this arc.

They advanced into the crevasse between the two hills; when they came within 34 m (112 ft) of the Russian guns on the Mühlberge, they charged at point-blank range. Some of Shuvalov's Observation Corps, stationed on the summit, took substantial losses—perhaps 10 percent—before the Prussian grenadiers overwhelmed them. Prussian losses were also high. Frederick sent 4,300 men into this assault, immediately losing 206 of Prince Henry's cuirassiers.

Although Saltykov sent his own grenadiers to shore up the Russian defense, the Prussians carried the Mühlberge, capturing between 80 and 100 enemy cannons, which they immediately deployed against the Russians. For the moment, the Prussians held the position.

After capturing the cannons, the Prussians raked the retreating Russians with fire from their own pieces. The Russians were slaughtered by the score, losing most of five large regiments to injury and death. By 1:00 pm, the Russian left flank had been defeated and driven back on Kunersdorf itself, leaving behind small, disorganized groups capable of only token resistance.

In panic, some of the Russians even fired on the Margrave of Baden-Baden's troops, which also wore blue coats (although of a lighter blue), mistaking them for Prussians. Saltykov fed in more units, including a force of Austrian grenadiers led by Major Joseph De Vins, and gradually the situation stabilized.

ATTACK STALLED

The Prussian position at Kunersdorf was not substantially better than it had been a few hours earlier, but it was, at least, defensible; the Russian position, on the other hand, was substantially worse. While Frederick's principal force had assaulted the Mühlberge, Johann Jakob von Wunsch, with 4,000 men, had retraced his steps from Reitwein to Frankfurt and had captured the city by midday. The Prussians had effectively blocked the Allies from moving east, west or south, and the terrain blocked them from moving north; if they tried such a foolhardy move, Moller's artillery would rake them with enfilade fire.

The King's brother, Prince Henry, and several other generals encouraged Frederick to stop there. The Prussians could defend Frankfurt from their vantage point on the Mühlberge and in the city itself. To descend into the valley, cross the Kuhgrund and ascend Spitzberge against frightful fire was foolhardy, they argued. Furthermore, the weather was blisteringly hot and the troops had endured forced marches to reach the theater and the battlefield. They were exhausted and low on water. The men had not had a hot meal in several days, having bivouacked the night before without fires.

Despite these arguments, Frederick wanted to press his initial success. He had won half the battle and wanted the whole victory. He decided to continue the fight. He transferred his artillery to the Mühlberge, and ordered Finck's battalions to assault the Allied salient from the northwest, while his main strike force would cross the Kuhgrund. To complete Frederick's battle plan, the Prussians would have to descend from the Mühlberge to the lower Kuhgrund, cross the spongy field, and then assault the well-defended higher ground. This is where Saltykov had concentrated his men, making the Grosser Spitzburg nearly impregnable. At this point in his plan, Frederick intended to have the second half of a pincer movement ready to squeeze the Russian left.

The rearmost forces were supposed to have advanced straight against the Russians from the south, while the right wing did the same from the north. The right was where it was supposed to be, with the exception of one of the support formations for the right wing, which was held up by mis-information about the ground: a couple of bridges that crossed the Huhner Fleiss were too narrow for the artillery teams.

The left was still out of position. Anticipating Frederick's plan, Saltykov had reinforced the salient with reserves from the west and southwest; these reserves included most of Laudon's fresh infantry. Finck made no progress at the salient and the Prussian attack at the Kuhgrund was thwarted with murderous fire along their very narrow front. Watching from the luxury of the Kleiner Spitzberge immediately east of the village, Saltykov judiciously fed in reinforcements from other sectors, and awaited results. Once, in the fierce fighting, it looked like the Prussians might break through, but gradually the Allied superiority of 423 artillery pieces could be brought to bear on the struggling Prussians. The Allied grenadiers held their lines. The Prussian left had been held up by a variety of problems, mostly relating to the inadequately-scouted terrain.

Two small ponds and several streams trisected the ground between the Prussian front and the Russians, which the Russians had also littered with abatis. This required the Prussian line to break into small columns that could march along narrow passages between the water and marshy ground, diminishing the legendary fire-power of the Prussian line of attack. Outside the shtetl, the Prussians tried to break through the Russian line; they got as far as the Jewish cemetery at the eastern base of Judenberge, but lost two thirds of Krockow's 2nd Dragoons in the process: 484 men and 51 officers gone in minutes. The 6th Dragoons lost another 234 men and 18 officers as well. Other regiments battling through the Russians and the terrain had comparable losses. Despite these problems, they continued to slog through the Russian positions, advancing toward the Kuhgrund outside what remained of Kunersdorf's wall.

CAVALRY ATTACK

The battle culminated in the early evening hours with a Prussian cavalry charge, led by von Seydlitz, upon the Russian center and artillery positions, a futile effort. The Prussian cavalry suffered heavy losses from cannon fire and retreated in complete disorder. Seydlitz himself was badly wounded and, in his absence, Generalleutnant Dubislav Friedrich von Platen assumed command. Under Frederick's orders, Platen organized a last-ditch effort. His scouts had discovered a crossing past the chain of ponds south of Kunersdorf, but it lay in full view of the artillery batteries on the Grosser Spitzberge. Seydlitz, still following the action, noted that it was foolish to charge a fortified position with cavalry. His assessment was correct, but Frederick had apparently lost his ability to think objectively. The strength of Frederick's cavalry lay in its ability to attack at a full gallop, with riders knee to knee and horses touching at the shoulders.

The units sent against the position shattered; they had to attack piecemeal because of the manner in which the ground was naturally formed. Before any further action could take place, Laudon himself led the Austrian cavalry's counter-attack around the obstacles and routed Platen's cavalry.

The fleeing men and horses trampled their own infantry around the base of the Mühlberge. General panic ensued. The cavalry attack against fortified positions had failed. The Prussian infantry had been on its feet for 16 hours, half of that in a forced march over muddy and uneven terrain, and the other half in slogging battle against formidable odds, in hot weather.

Despite the apparent futility, the Prussian infantry repeatedly attacked the Spitzberge, each time with greater losses; the 37th Infantry lost 992 men and 16 officers, more than 90 percent of its force. The King himself led two attacks of the 35th Infantry, and lost two of his horses in the effort.

He was mounting a third when the animal was shot in the neck and fell to the ground, nearly crushing the King. Two of Frederick's adjutants pulled him from under the horse as it fell.

A ball smashed the gold snuff box in his coat, and this box, plus his heavy coat, probably saved his life.

EVENING ACTION

By 5:00 pm, neither side could make any gains; the Prussians held tenaciously to the captured artillery works, too tired to even retreat: they had pushed the Russians from the Mühlberge, the village, and the Kuhgrund, but no further. The Allies were in a similar state, except they had more cavalry in reserve and some fresh Austrian infantry.

This part of Laudon's forces, late arrivals to the scene and largely unused, came into action at about 7:00 pm. To the exhausted Prussians holding the Kuhgrund, the swarm of fresh Austrian reserves was the final stroke. Although such isolated groups as Hans Sigismund von Lestwitz's regiment put up a bold front, these groups lost heavily and their stubborn defense could not stop the chaos of the Prussian retreat. Soldiers threw their weapons and gear aside and ran for their lives.

The battle was lost for Frederick—it had actually been lost for the Prussians for a couple of hours—but he had not accepted this fact. Frederick rode among his melting army, snatched a regimental flag, trying to rally his men: *Children, my children, come to me. Avec moi, Avec moi!*

They did not hear him, or if they did, they chose not to obey. Watching the chaos and seeking the *coup de grâce*, Saltykov threw his own Cossacks and Kalmyks (cavalry) into the fray.

The Chuggavieski Cossacks surrounded Frederick on a small hill, where he stood with the remnants of his body-guard—the Leib Cuirassiers—determined to either hold the line or to die trying. With a 100-strong hussar squadron, Rittmeister (cavalry captain) Joachim Bernhard von Prittwitz-Gaffron cut his way through the Cossacks and dragged the King to safety. Much of his squadron died in the effort.

As the hussars escorted Frederick from the battlefield, he passed the bodies of his men, lying on their faces with their backs slashed open by Laudon's cavalry. A dry thunderstorm created a surreal effect.

AFTERMATH

That evening back in Reitwein, Frederick sat in a peasant hut and wrote a despairing letter to his old tutor, Count Karl-Wilhelm Finck von Finckenstein: This morning at 11 o'clock I have attacked the enemy. ... All my troops have worked wonders, but at a cost of innumerable losses. Our men got into confusion. I assembled them three times. In the end I was in danger of getting captured and had to retreat. My coat is perforated by bullets, two horses of mine have been shot dead. My misfortune is that I am still living ... Our defeat is very considerable: To me remains 3,000 men from an army of 48,000 men. At the moment in which I report all this, everyone is on the run; I am no more master of my troops. Thinking of the safety of anybody in Berlin is a good activity ... It is a cruel failure that I will not survive. The consequences of the battle will be worse than the battle itself. I do not have any more resources, and—frankly confessed—I believe that everything is lost. I will not survive the doom of my fatherland. Farewell forever! Frederick also decided to turn over command of the army to Finck. He told this unlucky general he was sick. He named his brother as generalissimo and insisted his generals swear allegiance to his nephew, the 14-year-old Frederick William.

CASUALTIES

Before the battle, both armies had been reinforced by smaller units; by the time of the battle, the Allied forces had about 60,000 men, with another 5,000 holding Frankfurt, and the Prussians had almost 50,000. The Russians and Austrians lost about 15,000 men (approx. 5,000 killed), although some sources suggest a slightly higher number, perhaps 15,600 or 15,700, about 26 percent. Christopher Duffy places Russian losses at 13,477; in addition, the Russians had lost about 4,000 at the Battle of Kay a week earlier. Sources differ on Prussian losses. Duffy maintains 6,000 killed and 13,000 wounded, a casualty rate of more than 37 percent. Gaston Bodart represents losses at 39 percent, and that two thirds (12,000) of the 19,000 casualties were deaths. Frank Szabo places Prussian losses at 21,000. Following the battle, the victorious Cossack troops plundered corpses and slit the throats of the wounded; this no doubt contributed to the death rate. The Prussians lost their entire horse artillery, an amalgam of cavalry and artillery in which the crews rode horses into battle, dragging their cannons behind them, one of Frederick's notable inventions. The Prussians also lost 60 percent of their cavalry, killed or wounded, animals and men. The Prussians lost 172 of their own cannons plus the 105 that they had captured from the Russians in the late morning on the Mühlberge. They also lost 27 flags and two standards. Staff losses were significant. Frederick lost eight regimental colonels. Of his senior command, Seydlitz was wounded and had to relinquish command to Platen, nowhere near his equal in energy and nerve; Wedel was wounded so badly that he never fought again; Georg Ludwig von Puttkamer, commander of the Puttkamer Hussars, lay among the dead.

Friedrich Wilhelm von Steuben, later the inspector general and major general of the Continental Army during the American Revolutionary War, was wounded at the battle. Ewald Christian von Kleist, the famous poet of the Prussian army, was badly injured in the latter moments of the assault on the Walkeberge. By the time he was injured, Major Kleist was the highest-ranking officer in his regiment. Generalleutnant August Friedrich von Itzenplitz died of his wounds on 5 September, Prince Charles Anton August von Holstein-Beck on 12 September, and Finck's brigade commander, Generalmajor George Ernst von Klitzing, on 28 October in Stettin. Prussia was at its last gasp and Frederick despaired of preserving much of his remaining kingdom for his heir.

RAID ON BERLIN

The **Raid on Berlin** took place in October 1760 during the Third Silesian War (part of the Seven Years' War) when Austrian and Russian forces occupied the Prussian capital of Berlin for several days. After raising money from the city, and with the approach of further Prussian reinforcements, the occupiers withdrew. There were later allegations that the Russian commander Count Tottleben had received a personal bribe from the Prussians to spare the city, and he was subsequently tried and found guilty of being a spy.

BACKGROUND

After a series of successes over Prussian forces in 1759, the following year proved to be a disappointment for the Allies as their invasion of Silesia had stalled, in spite of their overwhelming manpower, and they had been defeated at the Battle of Liegnitz in August 1760. However, the Prussian capital, Berlin had been left vulnerable by Frederick the Great's decision to concentrate his forces in Silesia. This led to France suggest that Russia could make a lightning raid on Berlin, the Prussian capital. A smaller Austrian raid had briefly occupied the city in October 1757.

The plan drawn up by the allies envisaged a feint towards Guben by the main army, which would allow a force under Heinrich Tottleben to detach itself and hurry northwards to strike at Berlin. This would be followed a separate Austrian force under Count von Lacy. Large numbers of cossacks and light cavalry were to take part in the raid to give it added speed.

OCCUPATION

Tottleben led a vanguard of 5,600 Russians which crossed the River Oder and attempted to take the city by a coup de main on 5 October. This attempt to surprise the city failed in the face of unexpected opposition. The Governor of the city, General Hans Friedrich von Rochow wanted to withdraw in the face of the Russian threat, but the Prussian cavalry commander Friedrich Wilhelm von Seydlitz recovering from his wounds in the city, rallied the 2,000 defenders and managed to drive them back from the city gates. Having received word of the danger to Berlin, Prince Eugene of Württemberg led his troops back from fighting the Swedes in Pomerania while a contingent from Saxony also arrived, boosting the defenders to around 18,000. The arrival of Lacy's Austrians, however, swung the balance in favour of the Allies. The Austrians occupied Potsdam and Charlottenburg and in the face of these superior forces the Prussian defenders were forced to abandon the city and retreat to nearby Spandau.

On 9 October the City Council decided to surrender the city formally to the Russians rather than the Austrians, as Austria was Prussia's bitterest enemy. The Russians immediately made a demand for 4 million Thalers in exchange for the protection of private property. A prominent merchant Johann Ernst Gotzkowsky took over the negotiations on behalf of Berlin, and was able to persuade Tottleben to reduce the levy to 1.5 million Thalers, Meanwhile, the Austrians had forced their way into the city and occupied large parts of it.

The Austrians were more keen to exact revenge on the city because of Prussian behavior in occupied Saxony and on Austrian territory. The Russians, represented by First Major John O'Rourke, were concerned about improving their international reputation generally acted with greater restraint and emphasized respect towards the inhabitants.Several areas of the city were ransacked by the occupiers, and several royal palaces were burnt. Around 18,000 muskets and 143 cannons were seized. Austrian and Russian Battle flags, captured during fighting, were retaken and around 1,200 prisoners of war were released. Frederick was particularly worried about the paintings and books in his palace: one of his agents reported to him that the Russians had taken some, but the murals and gilding were fine, and only a few of the marble statues knocked over. The Austrians took about 130 11 and 12 year old cadets captive, from the military school, and held them in Koenigsberg until the end of the war. The troops did manage to destroy parts of the foundry .

WITHDRAWAL

A rumour that Frederick the Great was marching to the rescue of Berlin with his superior forces prompted the commanders to withdraw from the city as they had completed their major objectives. The occupiers withdrew from the city on 12 October, with the national contingents heading in separate directions. The Austrians under Lacy headed towards Saxony while the Russians rejoined their main army in the vicinity of Frankfurt.

Once he had realised that Berlin had now been abandoned by the enemy, Frederick halted his rescue attempt and turned back to concentrate on Silesia and Saxony.

AFTERMATH

Frederick was furious at the failure of his local forces and the inhabitants to actively resist the invaders. However, despite the loss of prestige, the raid was not especially significant for the military. In the wake of the occupation, the Prussians under Frederick fought, and narrowly won, the Battle of Torgau. Tottleben was later accused of being a Prussian spy, and was sentenced to death - only to receive a pardon from Catherine the Great. In early 1762 Berlin came under the threat of more permanent and decisive occupation, but Frederick was spared by the Miracle of the House of Brandenburg.

TREATY OF SAINT PETERSBURG

The **Treaty of Saint Petersburg** was concluded on May 5, 1762, and ended the fighting in the Seven Years' War between Prussia and Russia. The treaty followed the accession of Emperor Peter III, who admired the Prussian king Frederick the Great. It allowed the latter to concentrate on his other enemies, Austria and Saxony, in what became known as the "Miracle of the House of Brandenburg." The treaty was signed on by Chancellor Vorontsov for Russia and for Prussia by its envoy, Baron Wilhelm Bernhard von der Goltz (de). Russia pledged to assist in concluding peace among the individual participants in the Seven Years' War and to return to Prussia all lands occupied by Russian troops during the war. The intent to return the land was made known before the signing of the treaty; on February 23, Russia declared "that there ought to be Peace with this King of Prussia; that Her Tsarish Majesty, for their own part, is resolved on the thing; gives up East Prussia and the so-called conquests made; Russian participation in such a War has ceased." Furthermore, it was agreed that Russia would help Prussia in negotiating a peace with Sweden. Frederick II (1712-1786) was so overjoyed, that he "ordered Te Deum and fêtes (festivals)" after the signing of the Treaty on May 5. His reason for rejoicing was well merited, "for the Tsar promised him assistance of a token force of 18,000 men" to be used against the Austrian army. The subsequent Treaty of Hubertusburg made peace between Prussia, Austria and Saxony, but "though it restored the prewar status quo, marked the ascendancy of Prussia as a leading European power." Two years after the treaty, Prussia and Russia would enter into a defensive alliance.

РИСУНКИ

ОДЕЖДЫ и ВООРУЖЕНІЯ

РОССІЙСКИХЪ

ВОЙСКЪ.

PLATES LIST OF ILLUSTRATIONS

334 Hussar of the yellow regiment in 1760 and 1761.

335 Musketeer of the Pandur regiment, from 1752 to 1763.

336 Grenadier of the Pandur Regiment, from 1752 to 1763.

337 Grenadier plaque on the Pandur hats, from 1732 to 1761.

338 Officer of the Pandur Regiment, from 1752 to 1763.

339 Officer and Grenadier of Novomirgorod Garrison, from 1760 to 1763.

340 Regimental Emblems.

341 Fusilier of the Artillery Regiment, in 1757 and 1758.

342 Artillery cartridge paddles, 1757 and 1758. Peltier and powder flask, from 1757 to 1761.

343 Cannoner of the Artillery Regiment, in 1757 and 1758.

344 Sergeant and NCO of the Artillery Regiment, in 1757 and 1758.

345 – 346 Bombardier Hats, from 1757 to 1761.

347 Bombardier Officer, in 1757 and 1758 years.

348 Bombardier drummer, in 1757 and 1758 years.

349 Furier meister of the Artillery regiment, from 1757 to 1762.

350 Fusilier Artillery and the Chief of the Engineer Regiment, in 1759, 1760 and 1761.

351 Sergeant L.-G. Preobrazhensky and Musketeers of L.-G. Semenovsky and Izmailovsky regiments, from 1742 to 1762.

352 – 357 Standard of L.-G. Preobrazhensky regiment, from 1742 to 1762. Cartridge Pouch of the Guards Grenadiers, from 1742 to 1762.

353 NCO of the regiments of the Life Guards: Preobrazhensky, Semenovsky and Izmailovsky, from 1742 to 1762.

354 Soldat and sergeant of Grenadier Company L.-G. Preobrazhensky regiment, from 1742 to 1762.

355 The Guards Grenadier Hat, from 1742 to 1762.

356 The Guards Grenadier Hat, from 1742 to 1762.

358 Guard Grenadier Officer, from 1742 to 1762.

359 – 361 Guards Officer Fusilier, from 1742 to 1761. Cartridge pouch of the Guards Grenadier Officers, from 1742 to 1762.

360 Ornaments of the Guards Officers' Fusilier, from 1742 to 1762.

362 Musician of L.-G. Semenovsky and Grenadier Drummer L.-G. Izmailovsky regiments, from 1742 to 1762.

363 Soldat of the L.G. The Horse Regiment, from 1742 to 1762.

364 Officer L.G. The Horse Regiment, from 1742 to 1762.

365 Grenadier Leib-Company, from 1742 to 1762 year.

366 – 370 Cartridge Pouch of Grenadiers of the Leib Company, from 1742 to 1762. Kavalergardsky Superwest, from 1742 to 1762.

367 Officer and Sergeant of the Life Company, from 1742 to 1762.

368 The drummer of the Leib Company, from 1742 to 1762.

369 Grenadier of the Leib company in the Cavalry Horse, from 1742 to 1762.

371 Officer of the Leib company in the Cavalry Horse, from 1742 to 1762.

372 – 373 The regimental banner of the regiment, which was not approved for the emblem, 1741-1761. The standard of the Life Company, December 31, 1741.

374 The banner of L.G. Preobrazhensky regiment, 1742 year.

375 Standard of the L.G. The Horse Regiment, 1742.

376 – 377 Banner of the Grenadier Regiment, March 30, 1756. Banner of the Musketeer Regiment of the Observation Corps, 1757.

378 – 379 Banner of the Land Cadet Corps, December 1760. Standard of the Land Cadet Corps, December 1760.

380 – 382 The banner of the Kalmyk Dragoon Company, March 2, 1748. Banner of the Artillery Regiment, 1757-1762.

381 Banners of the Zakamskii Landmilytsky Regiments, 8 April 1747

383 Timpanis Chariot of the Artillery Regiment, 1757-1762.

384 – 385 Timpani Chariot of the Artillery Regiment, 1757-1762.

386 – 387 Banner of the Azov Cossack Regiment, August 7, 1747. The Banner of the Chuguevsky Cossack Regiment, March 14, 1752.

388- 389 The Banner and the Badge of the Orenburg Cossacks, May 21, 1756.

390- Musketeer regiment in 1762.

The Russian Empress Elizabeth Petrovna

Musketeer of the Infantry Regiment, from 1756 to 1762. (In the summer dress uniform).

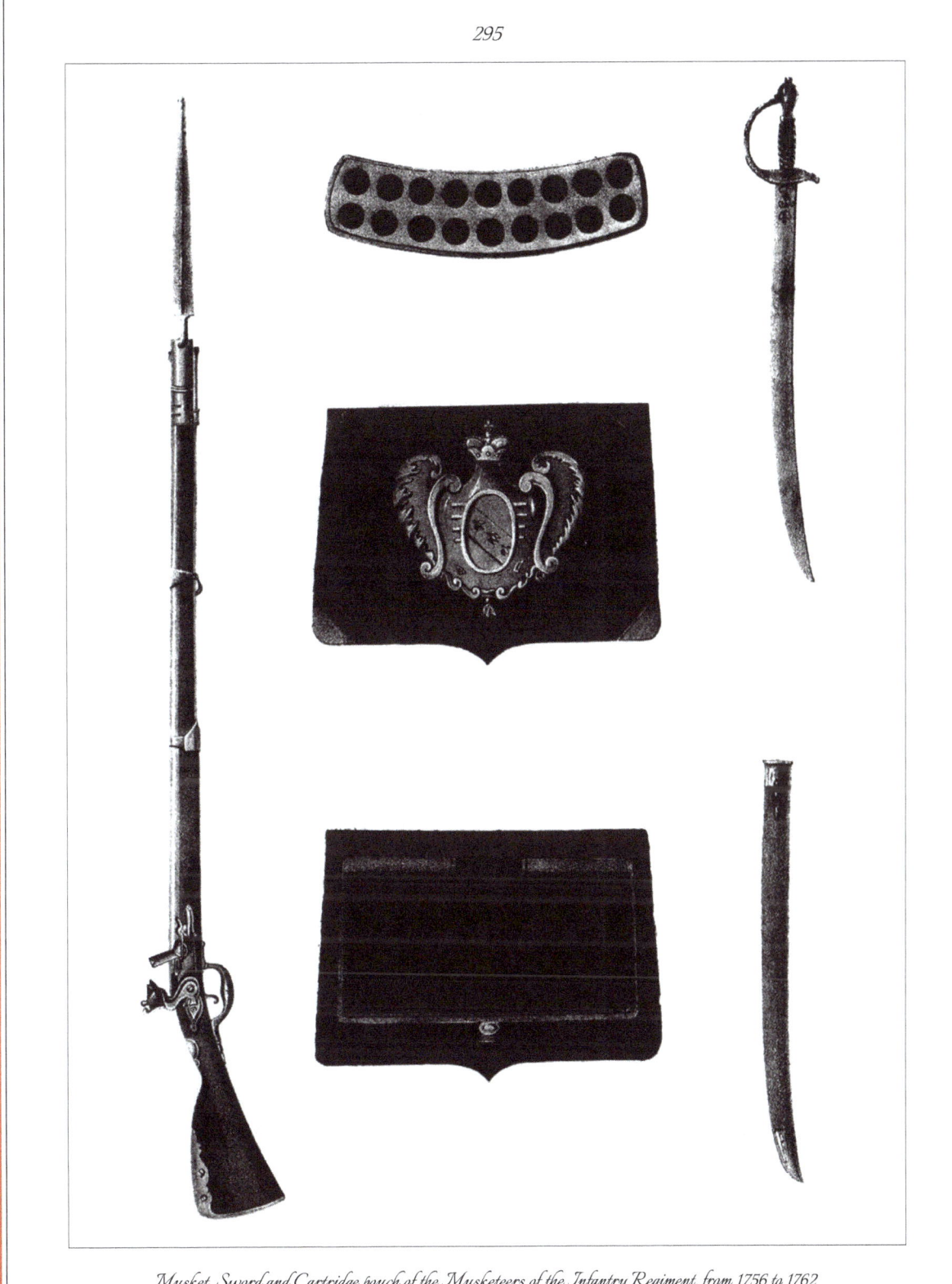

Musket, Sword and Cartridge pouch of the Musketeers of the Infantry Regiment, from 1756 to 1762.

Sergeant and Furier of the Infantry Regiment, from 1756 to 1762

Musketeers Officers of the infantry regiment, from 1756 to 1761. (In the all-day and in the dress uniform).

Rifle, Sword, Scarf, Badge and Pouch of Officers of the Infantry Regiment, from 1756 to 1762.

The HQ of the Infantry Regiment, from 1756 to 1761

300

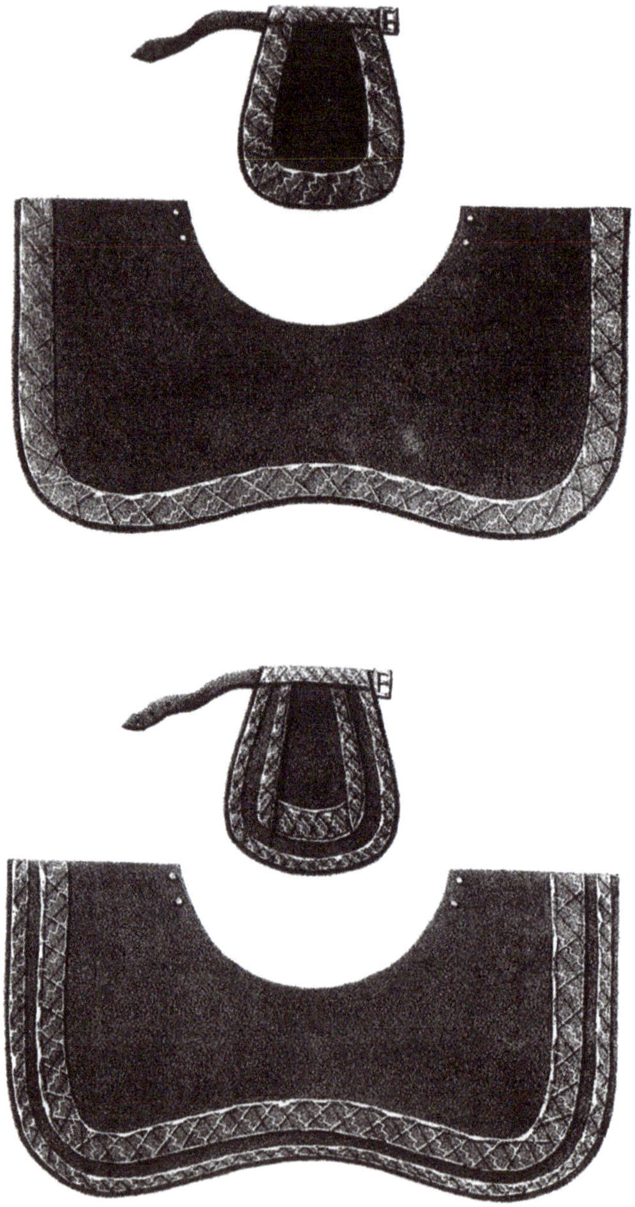

Shabraque of Staff-Officers Infantry Regiments, from 1756 to 1762. Cartridge Pouch of the Grenadiers of the Infantry Regiment, from 1756 to 1762.

Grenadier Infantry Regiment, from 1756 to 1762.

Mitria of Army Grenadiers, from 1756 to 1762.

Mitrias of Army Grenadiers, from 1756 to 1762

Shabraque of Staff-Officers Infantry Regiments, from 1756 to 1762. Cartridge Pouch of the Grenadiers of the Infantry Regiment, from 1756 to 1762.

Da fare da fare da fare

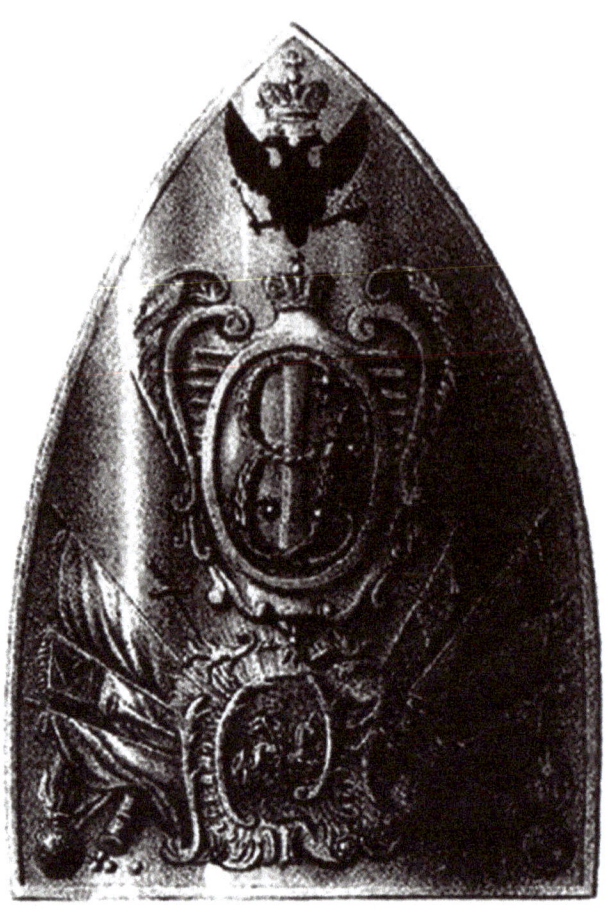

Grenadier Cartridge Pouch, from 1756 to 1761. The badge on the Grenadier's cap of Army Officers, from 1756 to 1762.

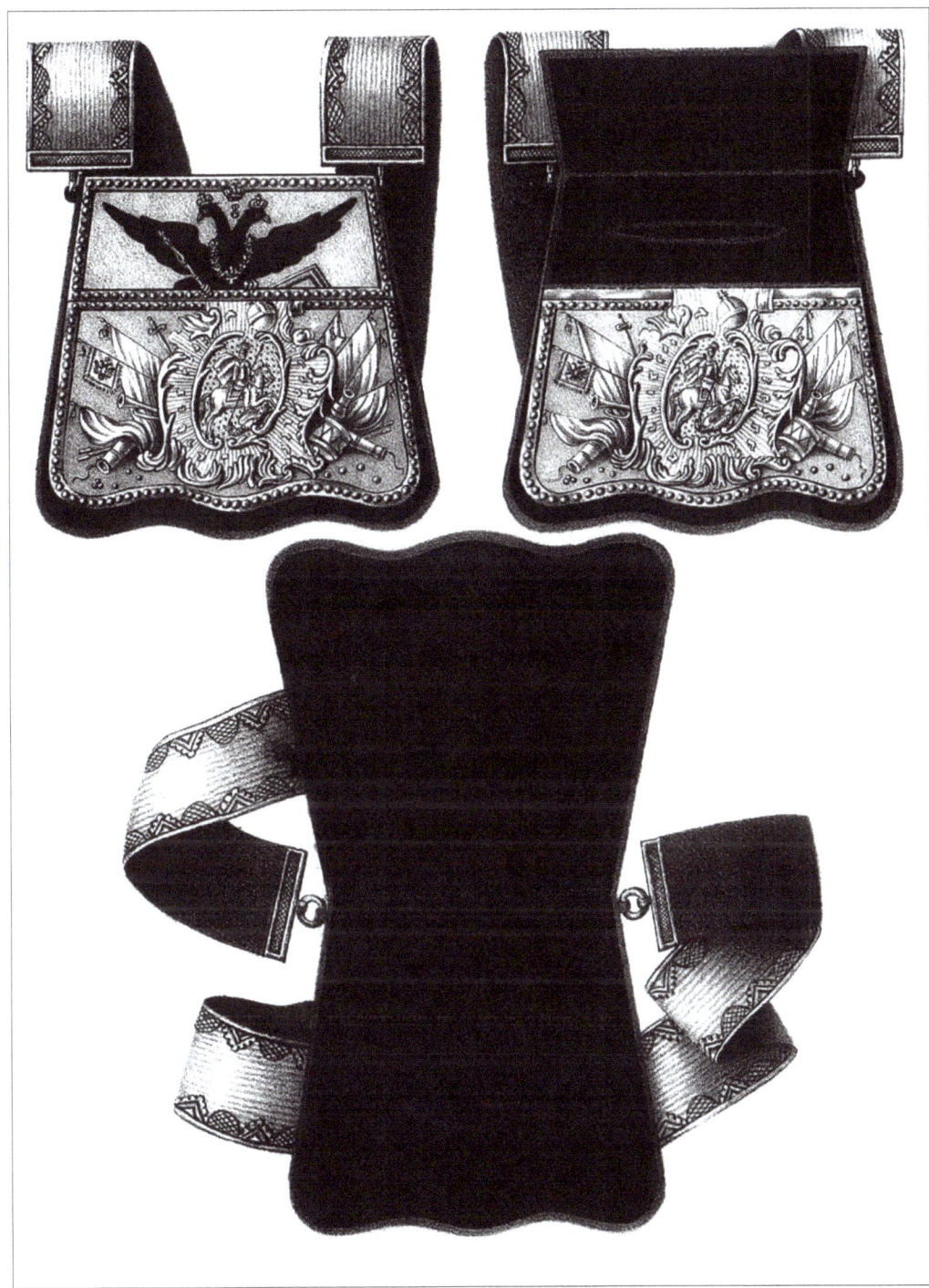

Grenadier Cartridge Pouch, from 1756 to 1761. The badge on the Grenadier's cap of Army Officers, from 1756 to 1762.

The drummer of the Grenadier Company of the infantry regiment, from 1756 to 1762

Oboist Infantry Regiment, from 1756 to 1762

Supervisor of Infantry Regiment, from 1756 to 1761

Musketeer of the Observational Corps, from 1756 to 1762

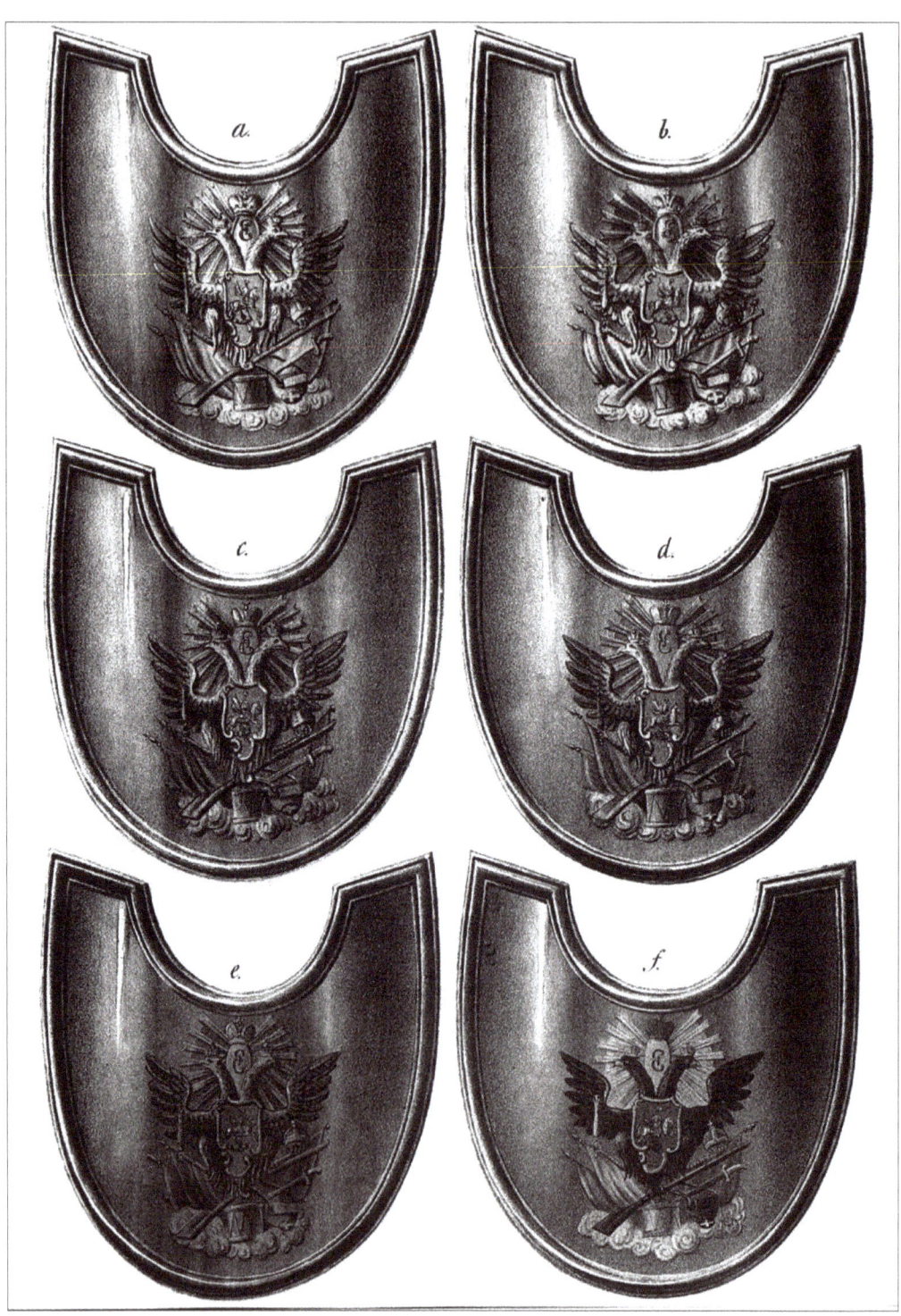

Officer signs of the regiments of the Observational Corps.

Dragoons from 1756 to 1761

Dragoons from 1756 to 1761

Palashi from 1756 to 1762. Shabraque of Staff Officers of the Dragoon Regiments, from 1756 to 1762

NCO of the Dragoon Company, from 1756 to 1761. The view depicts the time part of the building of the Twelve Colleges, in St. Petersburg.

Dragoons Officer from 1756 to 1761

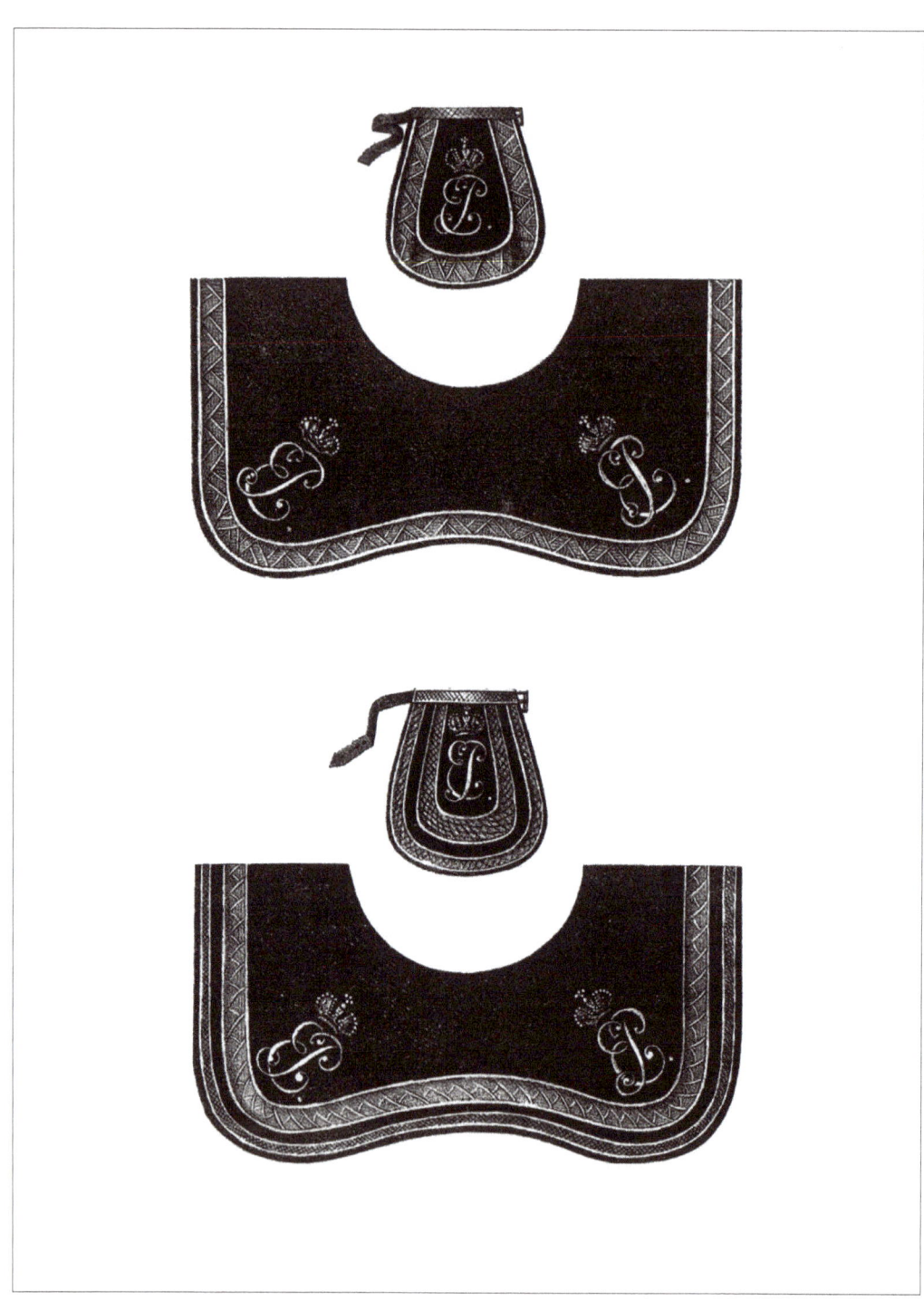

Palashi from 1756 to 1762. Shabraque of Staff Officers of the Dragoon Regiments, from 1756 to 1762

Horse grenadier, from 1756 to 1761

A horse-grenadier Officer, from 1756 to 1760. The view depicts the time part of St. Petersburg, from the left bank of the Fontanka River, near the present Anichkov Bridge.

Trumpeter of regiment cuirassier, from 1743 to 1745. (In the Formal dress).

Cuirassier from 1756 to 1762

NCO of the Cuirassier Regiment, from 1756 to 1761.

Officer of the Cuirassier Regiment, from 1756 to 1762. (In all-day dress).

Cornet of the Cuirassier regiment, from 1756 to 1762

Trumpeter of regiment cuirassier, from 1756 to 1761 year.

Hussar Serbian Regiment, from 1741 to 1761.

NCO of the Serbian Hussar Regiment, from 1741 to 1761

Officer of the Serbian Hussar Regiment, from 1741 to 1761

Hussar of the Hungarian Regiment, from 1741 to 1761

Officer of the Georgian Hussar Regiment, from 1741 to 1761

Hussar of the Georgian regiment, from 1741 to 1761.

Hussar Slobodsky Regiment, from 1756 to 1761

Hussar of the yellow regiment in 1760 and 1761

Musketeer of the Pandur regiment, from 1752 to 1763

Grenadier of the Pandur Regiment, from 1752 to 1763

Grenadier plaque on the Pandur hats, from 1732 to 1761.

Officer of the Pandur Regiment, from 1752 to 1763.

Officer and Grenadier of Novomirgorod Garrison, from 1760 to 1763.

Бахмутскаго
Гарнизоннаго баталіона.

Фридрихсгамскаго
Гарнизоннаго баталіона.

Чугуевскаго
Казачьяго полка.

Алексѣевскаго
Ландмилицкаго полка.

Сергіевскаго
Ландмилицкаго полка.

Билярскаго
Ландмилицкаго полка.

Шешминскаго
Ландмилицкаго полка.

Regimental Emblems.

Fusilier of the Artillery Regiment, in 1757 and 1758.

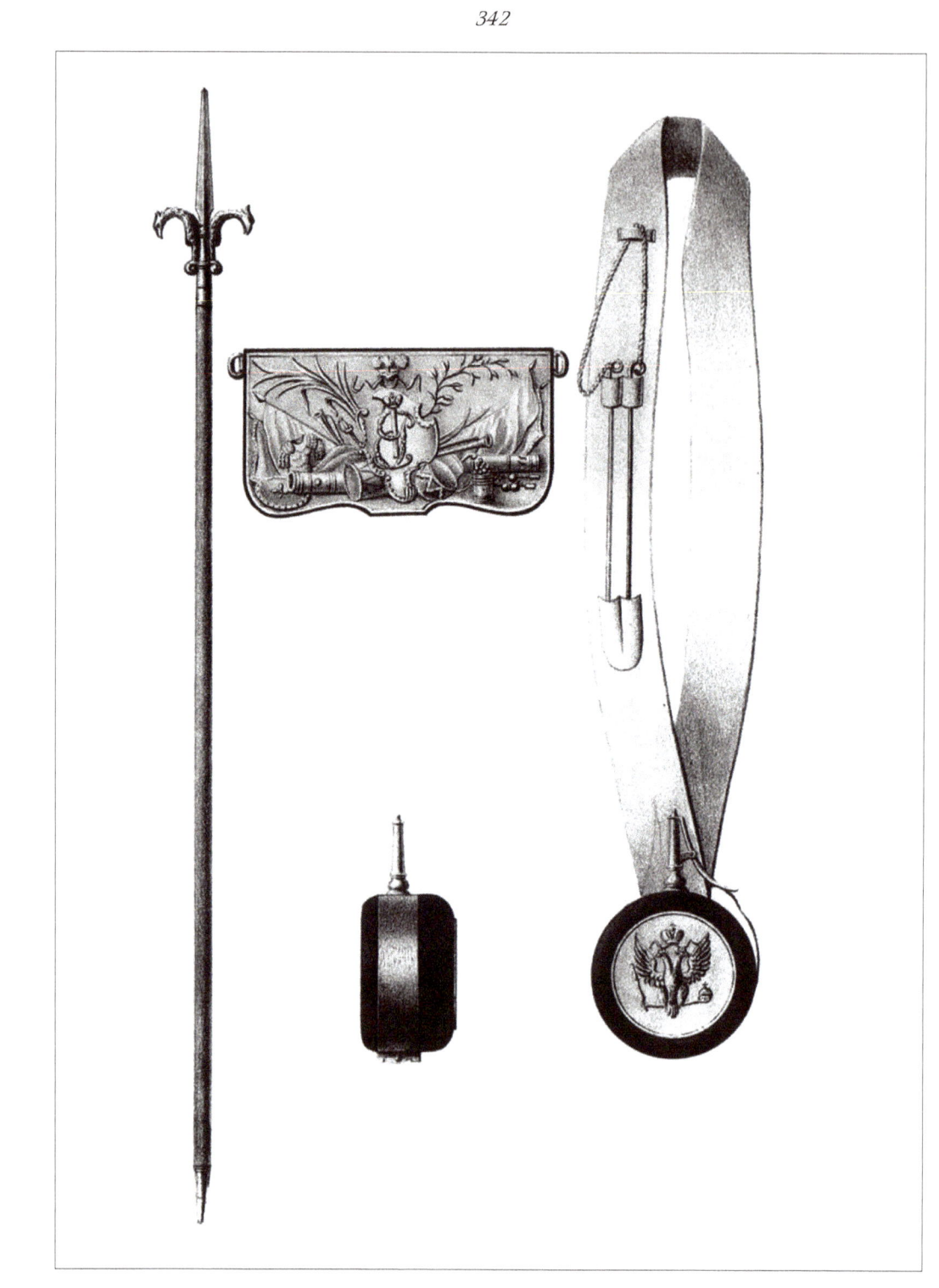

Artillery cartridge paddles, 1757 and 1758. Peltier and powder flask, from 1757 to 1761

Cannoner of the Artillery Regiment, in 1757 and 1758

Sergeant and NCO of the Artillery Regiment, in 1757 and 1758.

Bombardier Hats, from 1757 to 1761.

Bombardier Hats, from 1757 to 1761.

Bombardier Officer, in 1757 and 1758 years

347B

Bombardier Officer, in 1757 and 1758 years

Bombardier drummer, in 1757 and 1758 years

349

Furier meister of the Artillery regiment, from 1757 to 1762.

Fusilier Artillery and the Chief of the Engineer Regiment, in 1759, 1760 and 1761.

Sergeant L.-G. Preobrazhensky and Musketeers of L.-G. Semenovsky and Izmailovsky regiments, from 1742 to 1762.

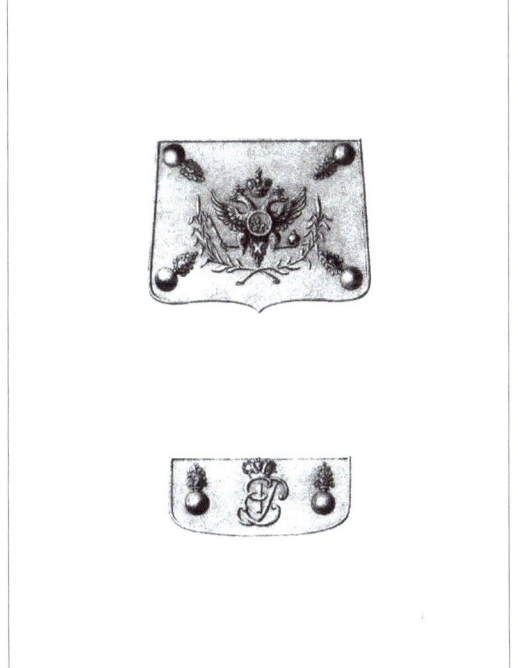

Standard of L.-G. Preobrazhensky regiment, from 1742 to 1762. Cartridge Pouch of the Guards Grenadiers, from 1742 to 1762

Guards Officer Fusilier, from 1742 to 1761. Cartridge pouch of the Guards Grenadier Officers, from 1742 to 1762

353

NCO of the regiments of the Life Guards: Preobrazhensky, Semenovsky and Izmailovsky, from 1742 to 1762

Soldat and sergeant of Grenadier Company L.-G. Preobrazhensky regiment, from 1742 to 1762.

The Guards Grenadier Hat, from 1742 to 1762

The Guards Grenadier Hat, from 1742 to 1762

Guard Grenadier Officer, from 1742 to 1762

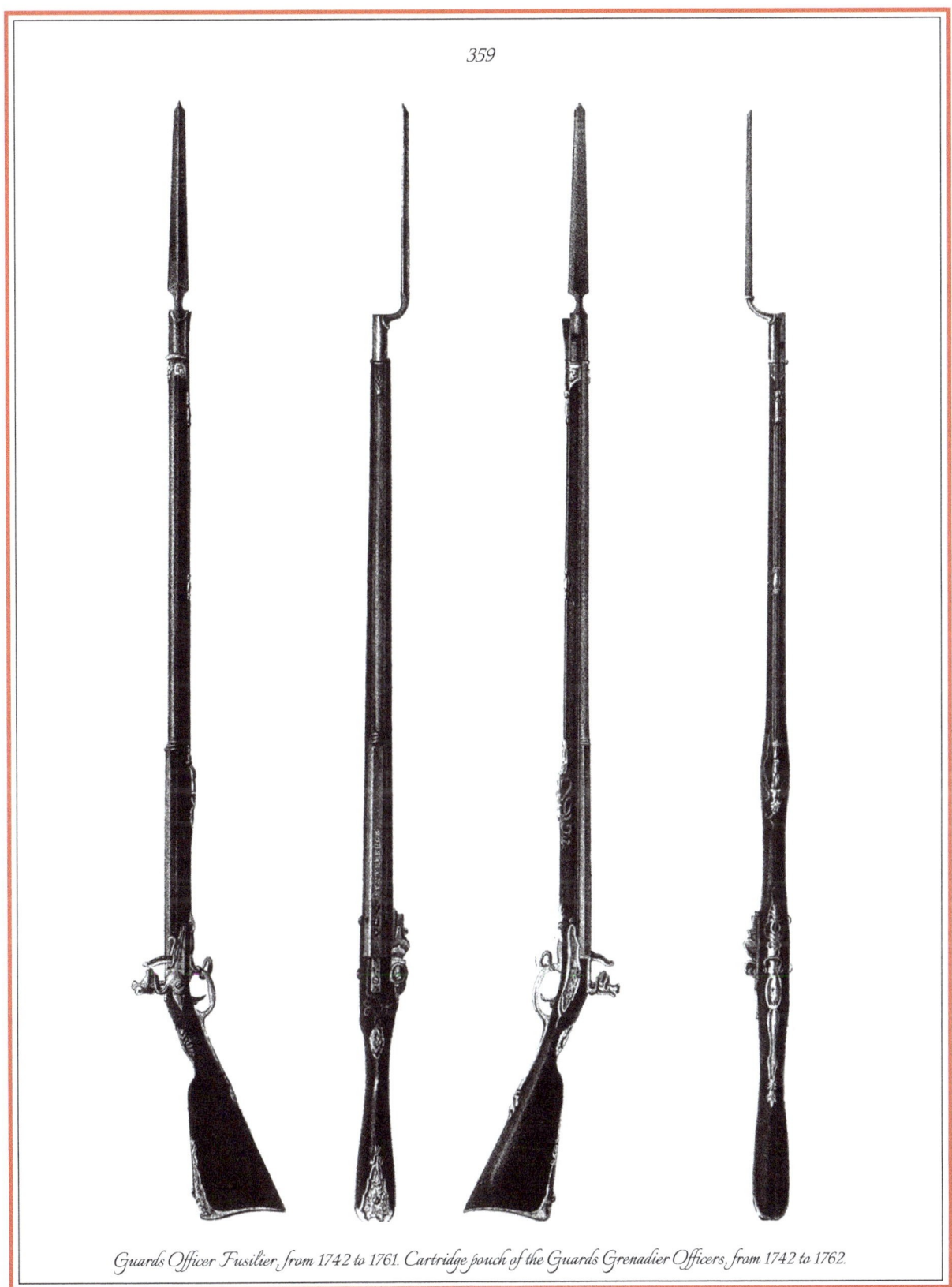

Guards Officer Fusilier, from 1742 to 1761. Cartridge pouch of the Guards Grenadier Officers, from 1742 to 1762.

Ornaments of the Guards Officers' Fusilier, from 1742 to 1762

Musician of L.-G. Semenovsky and Grenadier Drummer L.-G. Izmailovsky regiments, from 1742 to 1762

Soldat of the L.G. The Horse Regiment, from 1742 to 1762

Officer L.G. The Horse Regiment, from 1742 to 1762.

Grenadier Leib-Company, from 1742 to 1762 year

Cartridge Pouch of Grenadiers of the Leib Company, from 1742 to 1762. Kavalergardsky Superwest, from 1742 to 1762.

Officer and Sergeant of the Life Company, from 1742 to 1762.

368

The drummer of the Leib Company, from 1742 to 1762

Grenadier of the Leib company in the Cavalry Horse, from 1742 to 1762

Cartridge Pouch of Grenadiers of the Leib Company, from 1742 to 1762. Kavalergardsky Superwest, from 1742 to 1762.
Timpanis Chariot of the Artillery Regiment, 1757-1762

Officer of the Leib company in the Cavalry Horse, from 1742 to 1762

The regimental banner of the regiment, which was not approved for the emblem, 1741-1761. The standard of the Life Company, December 31, 1741.

The regimental banner of the regiment, which was not approved for the emblem, 1741-1761. The standard of the Life Company, December 31, 1741.

The banner of L.G. Preobrazhensky regiment, 1742 year

Standard of the L.G. The Horse Regiment, 1742
Banner of the Grenadier Regiment, March 30, 1756. Banner of the Musketeer Regiment of the Observation Corps, 1757.

Banner of the Grenadier Regiment, March 30, 1756. Banner of the Musketeer Regiment of the Observation Corps, 1757.

Banner of the Land Cadet Corps, December 1760. Standard of the Land Cadet Corps, December 1760.

Banner of the Land Cadet Corps, December 1760. Standard of the Land Cadet Corps, December 1760.

The banner of the Kalmyk Dragoon Company, March 2, 1748. Banner of the Artillery Regiment, 1757-1762

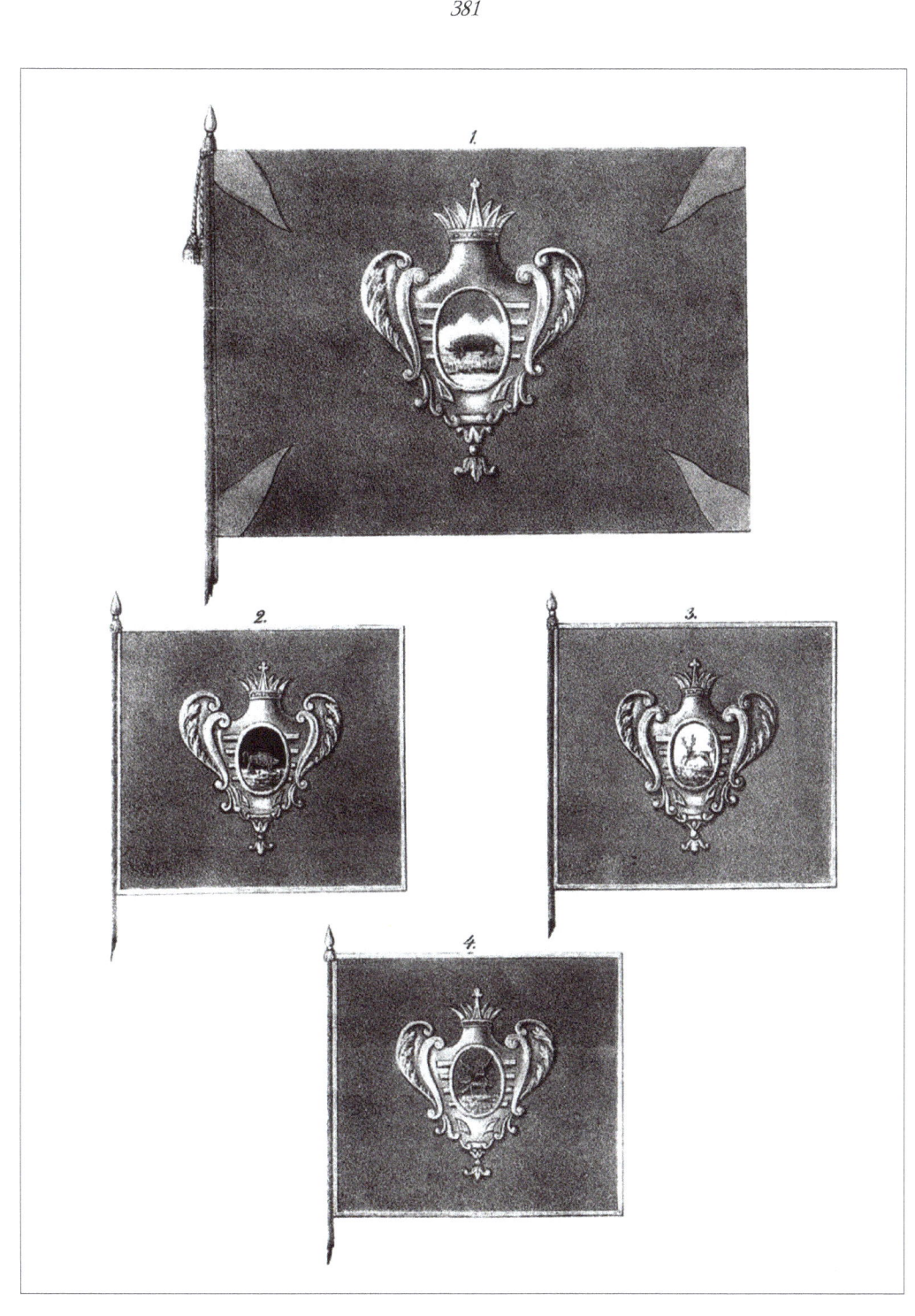

Banners of the Zakamskii Landmilytsky Regiments, 8 April 1747

TUETUR ET TERRET

The banner of the Kalmyk Dragoon Company, March 2, 1748. Banner of the Artillery Regiment, 1757-1762

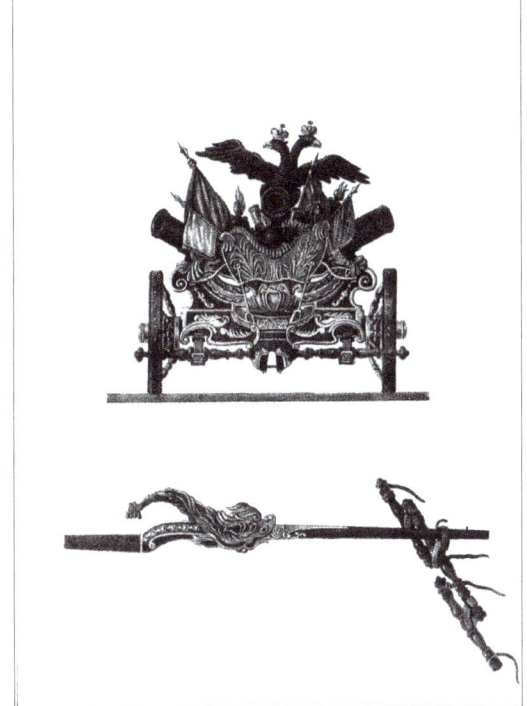

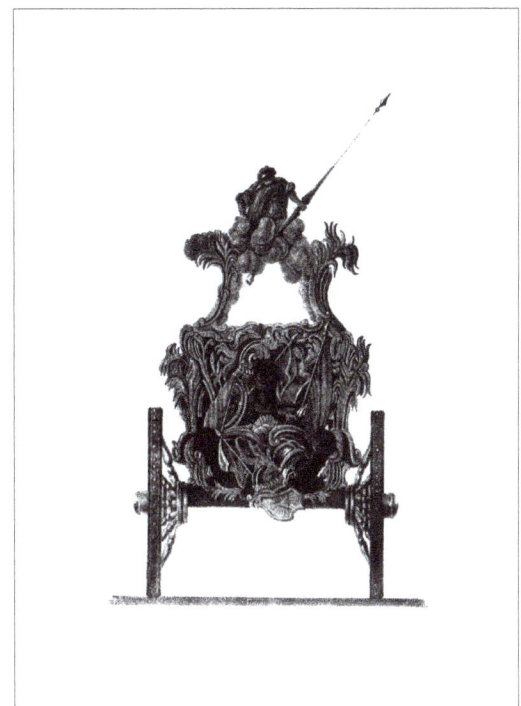

Timpani Chariot of the Artillery Regiment, 1757-1762
Banner of the Azov Cossack Regiment, August 7, 1747. The Banner of the Chuguevsky Cossack Regiment, March 14, 1752

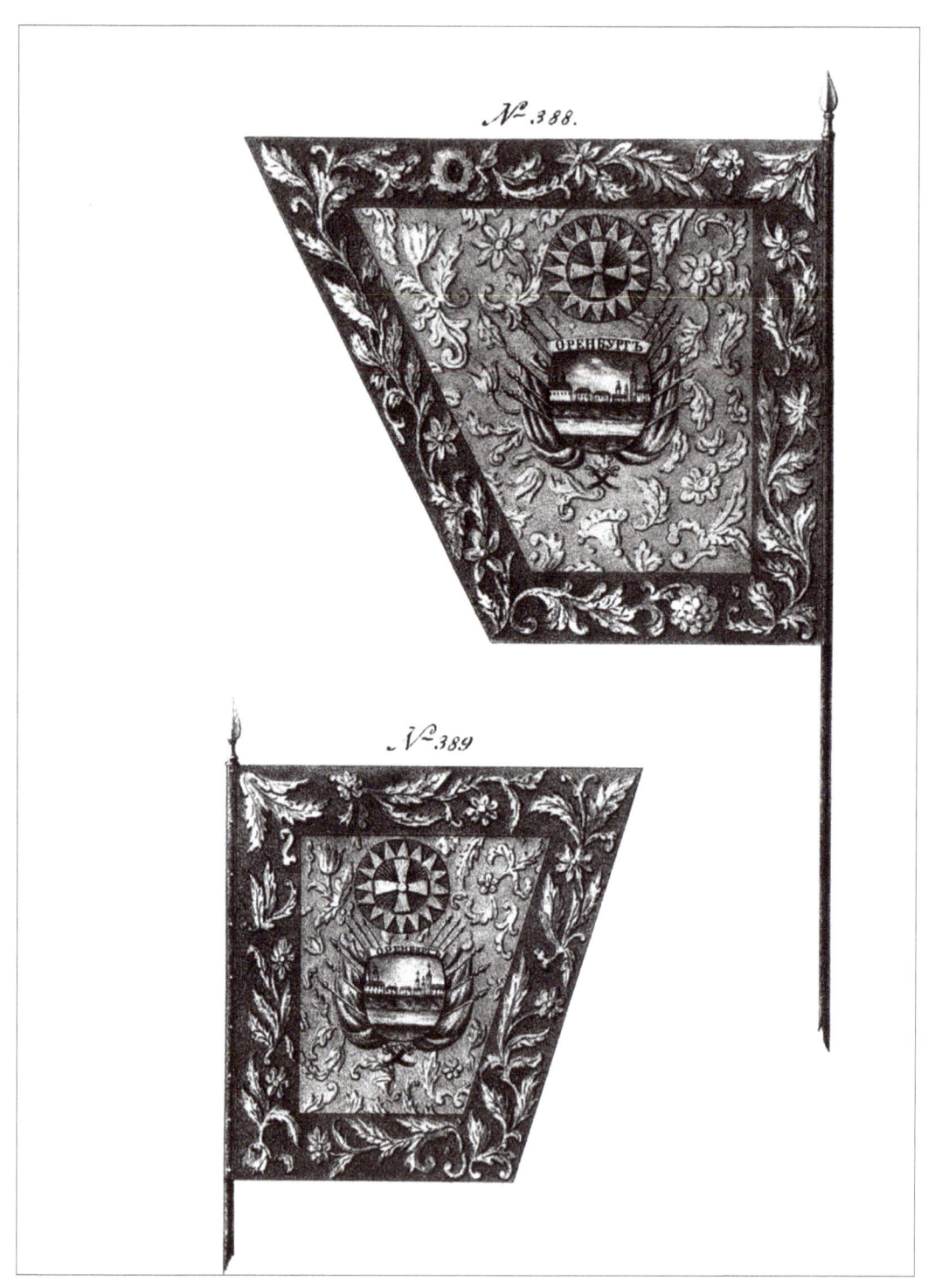

The Banner and the Badge of the Orenburg Cossacks, May 21, 1756

The Musketeers Regiment, in 1762

SOLDIERS, WEAPONS & UNIFORMS ALREADY PUBLISHED
(SOME TITLES)

UNIFORMS OF RUSSIAN ARMY IN THE ERA OF ANCIENT TZAR
FROM THE REIGN OF VASILI IV TO MICHAEL I, ALEXIS, FEODOR III DURING THE XVII th CENTURY
A.V.VISKOVATOV   LUCA STEFANO CRISTINI
SWU-600-004

UNIFORMS OF RUSSIAN ARMY OF PETER I THE GREAT
FROM THE REIGN OF PETER I TO CATHERINE I, PEER II, ANNA AND IVAN VI. 1682-1741
A.V.VISKOVATOV   LUCA STEFANO CRISTINI
SWU-700-006

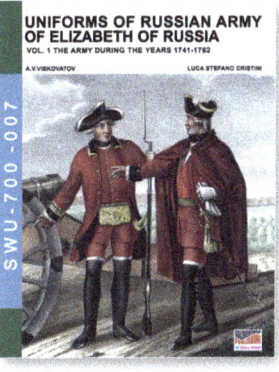

UNIFORMS OF RUSSIAN ARMY OF ELIZABETH OF RUSSIA
VOL. 1 THE ARMY DURING THE YEARS 1741-1762
A.V.VISKOVATOV   LUCA STEFANO CRISTINI
SWU-700-007

UNIFORMS OF RUSSIAN ARMY OF ELIZABETH OF RUSSIA
VOL. 2 THE ARMY DURING THE YEARS 1741-1762
A.V.VISKOVATOV   LUCA STEFANO CRISTINI
SWU-700-008

UNIFORMS OF RUSSIAN ARMY IN THE XVIII CENTURY VOL. 1
UNDER THE REIGN OF CATHERINE II EMPRESS OF RUSSIA BETWEEN 1762 AND 1796
A.V.VISKOVATOV – LUCA STEFANO CRISTINI
SWU-700-005

UNIFORMS OF RUSSIAN ARMY IN THE XVIII CENTURY VOL. 2
UNDER THE REIGN OF CATHERINE II EMPRESS OF RUSSIA BETWEEN 1762 AND 1796
A.V.VISKOVATOV – LUCA STEFANO CRISTINI
SWU-700-009

UNIFORMS OF RUSSIAN ARMY IN THE XVIII CENTURY VOL. 3
UNDER THE REIGN OF CATHERINE II EMPRESS OF RUSSIA BETWEEN 1762 AND 1796
A.V.VISKOVATOV – LUCA STEFANO CRISTINI
SWU-700-010

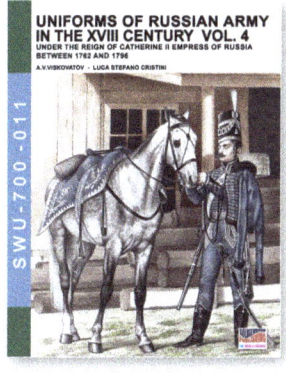

UNIFORMS OF RUSSIAN ARMY IN THE XVIII CENTURY VOL. 4
UNDER THE REIGN OF CATHERINE II EMPRESS OF RUSSIA BETWEEN 1762 AND 1796
A.V.VISKOVATOV – LUCA STEFANO CRISTINI
SWU-700-011

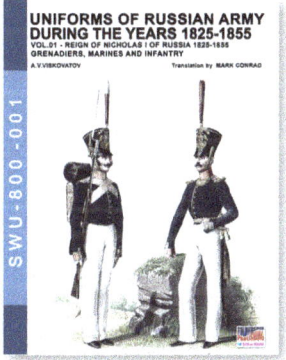

UNIFORMS OF RUSSIAN ARMY DURING THE YEARS 1825-1855
VOL.01 - REIGN OF NICHOLAS I OF RUSSIA 1825-1855 GRENADIERS, MARINES AND INFANTRY
A.V.VISKOVATOV   Translation by MARK CONRAD
SWU-800-001

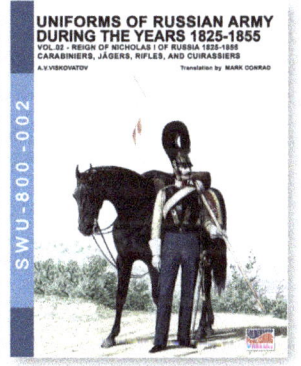

UNIFORMS OF RUSSIAN ARMY DURING THE YEARS 1825-1855
VOL.02 - REIGN OF NICHOLAS I OF RUSSIA 1825-1855 CARABINIERS, JÄGERS, RIFLES, AND CUIRASSIERS
A.V.VISKOVATOV   Translation by MARK CONRAD
SWU-800-002

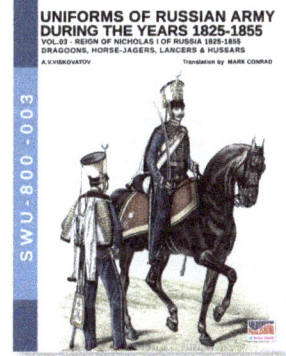

UNIFORMS OF RUSSIAN ARMY DURING THE YEARS 1825-1855
VOL.03 - REIGN OF NICHOLAS I OF RUSSIA 1825-1855 DRAGOONS, HORSE-JAGERS, LANCERS & HUSSARS
A.V.VISKOVATOV   Translation by MARK CONRAD
SWU-800-003

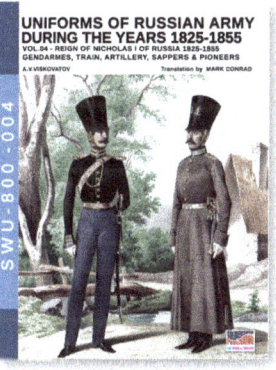

UNIFORMS OF RUSSIAN ARMY DURING THE YEARS 1825-1855
VOL.04 - REIGN OF NICHOLAS I OF RUSSIA 1825-1855 GENDARMES, TRAIN, ARTILLERY, SAPPERS & PIONEERS
A.V.VISKOVATOV   Translation by MARK CONRAD
SWU-800-004

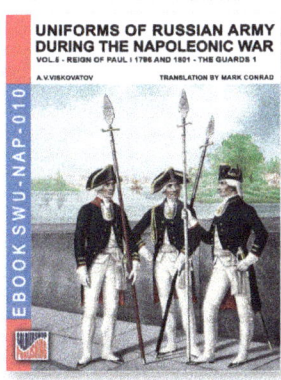

UNIFORMS OF RUSSIAN ARMY DURING THE NAPOLEONIC WAR
VOL.6 - REIGN OF PAUL I 1796 AND 1801 - THE GUARDS 1
A.V.VISKOVATOV   TRANSLATION BY MARK CONRAD
EBOOK SWU-NAP-010

UNIFORMS OF RUSSIAN ARMY DURING THE NAPOLEONIC WAR
VOL.10 - REIGN OF ALEXANDER I OF RUSSIA 1801-1825 CAVALRY: CUIRASSIERS, DRAGOONS & HORSE-JÄGERS
A.V.VISKOVATOV   Translation by MARK CONRAD
SWU-NAP-015

UNIFORMS OF RUSSIAN ARMY DURING THE NAPOLEONIC WAR
VOL.11 - REIGN OF ALEXANDER I OF RUSSIA 1801-1825 CAVALRY: HUSSARS, LANCERS, GENDARMES, & THE TRAIN
A.V.VISKOVATOV   Translation by MARK CONRAD
SWU-NAP-016

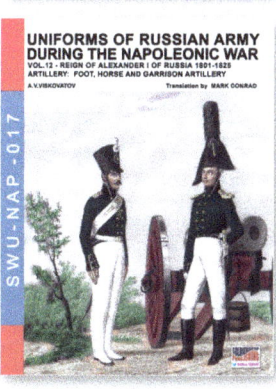

UNIFORMS OF RUSSIAN ARMY DURING THE NAPOLEONIC WAR
VOL.12 - REIGN OF ALEXANDER I OF RUSSIA 1801-1825 ARTILLERY: FOOT, HORSE AND GARRISON ARTILLERY
A.V.VISKOVATOV   Translation by MARK CONRAD
SWU-NAP-017